# CREATION

# CREATION

## AND THE HIGH SCHOOL STUDENT

compiled and edited by Kenneth N. Taylor

Tyndale House Publishers
Wheaton, Illinois

*cover: Tom Schmerler*
*design: Kathy Lay*
*Credits: pp. 5, 6, 10, 11, 12, 15, Lick*
*Observatory; p. 8, Youth for Christ*
*International; pp. 16, 18, H. Arm-*
*strong Roberts; p. 20, Stonnec from*
*Monkmeyer Press Photo Service;*
*pp. 23, 32, 34, Carol Hilk (after*
*Lessing); p. 24, Brookhaven National*
*Laboratory; p. 31, New York Times;*
*pp. 37, 43, 55, Gerard, from Monk-*
*meyer; pp. 38, 40, L. M. Beidlen from*
*Monkmeyer; p. 47, Gregor from*
*Monkmeyer; p. 51, Harrison from*
*Monkmeyer; pp. 52, 53, Watson from*
*Monkmeyer.*

Printed in the United States of America.

Do the heavens "declare the glory of God" as glowingly proclaimed by King David thousands of years ago? Or are they merely accident and happenstance? Your answer, whether right or wrong, can change your life.

Do you know that on a clear night you can see only as much of the universe as an amoeba can see of the ocean in which it drifts? All of the glory that the human eye can take in is comparable to its drop of water! Standing at night on the beach and being able to comprehend the vastness of the universe is as impossible as trying to count the grains of sand on which you are standing.

How did all of this grandeur originate? The Bible says, "The heavens declare the glory of God." That is, the stars exhibit His existence and power. But although the vastness of the universe should impress us, somehow it doesn't. We are used to it and just take it for granted. And though we can understand the argument that order and design among human beings postulate an orderer and designer, yet the thought seems strange that order and design in the heavens postulate a divine Doer. Who is this One who orders and designs our universe? Do we take Him for granted, too? Or do we just ignore Him, saying He doesn't exist?

When we see a hand-crafted cabinet we know it was made by a cabinet-maker. We have no difficulty at all in assuming this even though we did not see it made. Yet when we look up into the vastness of the universe and see stars moving in orderly relationship in vast interstellar space, we shrug our shoulders and express our inability even to guess how it all came about. We speak vaguely about chance and accident, or somehow, in the back of our minds, there is the thought that God must have done it, but it is so vast a miracle that we cannot really feel it, and no one else seems to notice it either, so the matter is forgotten. If

Examining the evidence is very important, but isn't really the first item on the agenda! Although the truth will become evident if one is open-minded, almost everyone begins with an assumption for or against God, thus biasing his interpretation of the evidence.

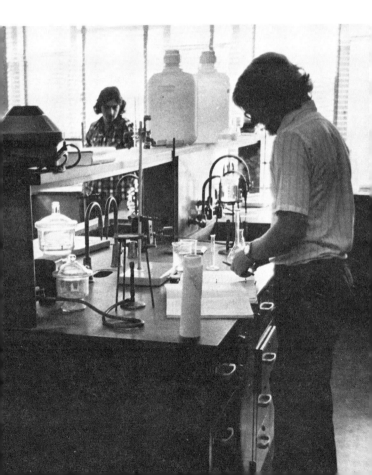

only our minds were not so dull or calloused! Would we not then recognize the universe as the handiwork of God and fall face downward in the dust in worship?

Why is the study of this subject important? Because if it is true that the heavens declare the glory of God, then here within our grasp is the key to an eternal mystery which leads us into the very presence of God. It is we who suffer loss (even though we may not be aware of it) if we ignore or turn away from the evidence for God's existence.

Our examination of the evidence begins with the macrocosm—the limitless distances of outer space. But how can we begin to take in its enormousness? The grandeur is beyond all comprehension. How shall we speak of the distance involved in one light year? For in a single year, light rushing out into space at the speed of 186,000 miles per second, travels six trillion (6,000,000,000,000) miles.

The sun is 860,000 miles across, compared with the earth's 8,000 miles— 100 times as wide! (If the sun were hollow, one million earths would easily fit inside.) But another star in our galaxy, Antares, is <u>150</u> <u>million</u> miles across. Into it would fit our entire solar system out to the orbit of Mars!

This cloud of stars is part of the universe of Sagittarius. Our own universe is 100,000 light years across and contains an estimated 100 billion other stars besides our sun. But ours is only one of a billion known universes.

Can you begin to see the glory of God and how the heavens show it to us?

This solar system of ours—the sun (which is a star) and its satellites—is part of a huge galaxy of 100 <u>billion</u> other stars formed into a giant pinwheel in space. Our solar system is out toward the edge of the pinwheel. It would take 100,000 years for light to travel from one end to the other, or 20,000 years through the thickness at the center. This giant pinwheel revolves "slowly" through space, with our solar system located in the part of the pinwheel traveling at the rate of 136 miles per second. Yet it takes 200 million years for the pinwheel to make one complete rotation.

When we look up at the Milky Way

we are looking into the pinwheel. The
far fewer stars we see beyond the edges
of the Milky Way are because we are
no longer looking into our galaxy, but
away from it, toward others.

Our earth is in a pinwheel galaxy somewhat like this one.
We are located in the part of the pinwheel rotating at a
speed of 136 miles per second. 200,000,000 years are required for one complete rotation.

But now think of this!  Our pin-wheel galaxy of billions of stars, 100,000 light years across, <u>is only one of a billion other</u> galaxies, some of them pinwheels, visible through telescopes from the earth!  The closest of these other universes is 200,000 light years away.  It is estimated that in addition to the billion universes we can see, there are other billions beyond our sight and comprehension, each containing hundreds of millions or billions of sun-sized stars.  Sir James Jeans has suggested that the number of stars in all the universes may equal the number of grains of sand lying on all the seashores of the world.  Some of these other constellations of stars out at the edge of space (by which we mean the farthest visible to our observation systems) are apparently moving away at a rate of millions of miles an hour, almost at the speed of light.

And far out beyond the farthest reaches of our imagination, who is to know whether space goes on and on a

billion times as far? And where does
it end? Are there *no* <u>boundaries</u>? And
did all this happen by chance?

*Limitless* space? *Never* ending? *No* boundaries? All the evidence points in that direction.

But though the stars number in the billions, yet space is almost empty! If our sun were the size of the dot over this "i," the nearest star in our pinwheel galaxy would be a dot ten miles away and other stars would be up to the size of a dime, hundreds and thousands of miles distant.

And now the question is, are these vastnesses of space—these never-ending distances, these eternities of time—are they mere chance formations or are they in a majestic order created by God? In other words, are they meaningless, or full evidence that confirms the existence of God?

The answer is extremely important. For if God exists, then you and I have a responsibility to know about Him—and to love and worship Him. But if the universe originated through chance and there is no Creator, then nothing in this universe or in our lives has purpose. All is accident and chance and we can "eat, drink and be merry," for there is no tomorrow and today is not valid. We are lost in the vast reaches of eternity, on a tiny planet, among a trillion stars. (What horror if God should lose track of the earth—a grain of sand lost upon the seashores of the world!)

We are not playing games. These incredible facts are real. Yet how many people blithely ignore them and go about their business, each to his own little way as though nothing else mattered—neither time, nor eternity, nor space, nor a billion billion stars a million times as big as the earth, nor never-ending space, nor God.

Yet the Bible says that God created it all: "By the Word of God the heavens were of old," and "Without Him nothing was created," and "In the beginning God created the heavens and the earth."

How do people come to the conclusion that the universes are mere accident and chance despite the enormous complexity of their movements, balance and interaction? Such people begin with the presupposition that

Good minds, good teachers, good textbooks—all are important. But the decisive factor of truth may never be ours unless we are willing to recognize the fact of God behind all nature. If He is there, and we ignore Him, our system is false.

there is no God. Then they say, "Since there is no God, then everything must be by accident and chance." This is what is known as circular reasoning and begging the question. Is it not more reasonable to declare accident and chance unlikely or impossible, and to presuppose God?

The microscopic world becomes increasingly complex as it is magnified. The most powerful student microscope barely "scratches the surface." Much of what we know about the invisible worlds of molecules, atoms, and electrons is by theory and calculation.

## 22  *The Big Bang?*

Not many theories have been suggested as to how the universe began. The "big bang" theory is currently the most popular. This theory postulates that sometime in the inconceivable past, billions and billions of years ago, vast fields of gas (where it came from, no one can guess) gradually condensed and finally became incandescent. Then, perhaps set off by heat, a blast occurred that shot the galaxies into space at inconceivable speeds. These whirling masses of molten universes have been rushing out through eternity ever since—for possibly five billion years. The galaxies farthest out, billions of light years away, move at

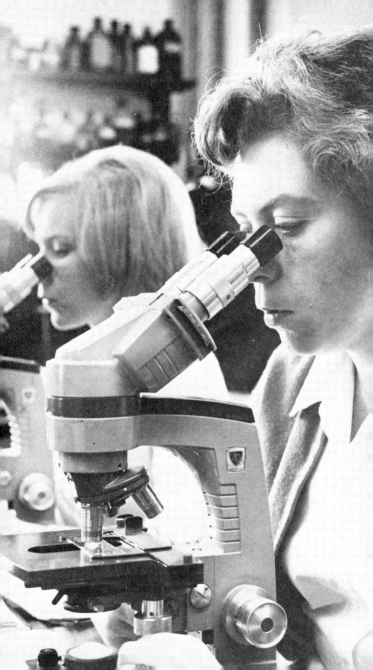

the greatest speed, at almost the speed of light.

The other main theory has been that of Fred Hoyle: the steady-state idea. He postulates that matter is constantly developing from nothing, continues for a few billions of years, and then disappears again into nothing. But in recent months Dr. Hoyle has himself begun to doubt the validity of this idea.

How it all came about—whether by a "steady-state" or a "big bang," or an instantaneous calling into existence—whatever the means, the incredible greatness of Someone's power is evident. Do not hesitate to let the wonder of it fill you with praise and admiration and worship. That we don't know how it was done is irrelevant. It is the fact that matters. Yet some people find this fact too incredible to believe. How would it be conceivable that there could be a billion universes in infinite space with no ultimate walls? Impossible, yes, but true. There it is—right up above us in the sky. If this is the work of God, He must be great indeed.

Human bloodcells

And now let us turn to the other side of the universe, to the world of plants and animals and cells, of molecules, atoms, protons, neutrons, and electrons—and who knows what else may be discovered in even tinier dimensions— contrasting immensely with the enormous worlds overhead.

In order for man to see these microcosmic elements they must be magnified by powerful microscopes just as the macrocosm around and beyond the earth must be magnified and brought closer by powerful telescopes. Although the contrast in the size of these two worlds is indeed great, many similarities exist between them.

The atom. Electrons in random orbits circle the nucleus billions of times in millionths of seconds!

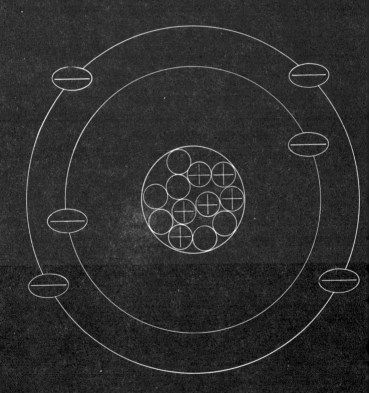

The electrons surrounding the nucleus in an atom are worlds apart, as far apart in proportion to their size as the planets are from the sun. And the electrons move in orbits (though random) just as the planets do. Electrons whirl around the atom's nucleus at fantastic speeds. They complete billions of trips around the nucleus in millionths of a second!

Amazing, incredible, glorious, fantastic.

Chance?

Accident?

Everything you see is made up of atoms—your chair, the floor, the wall, this book, the air you breathe, your body. Each consists of billions and billions of atoms so tiny no one can see them, yet so vast that there is a universe between their component parts.

Since it is true that atoms are mostly empty space dotted occasionally by weightless electrons with great distances between, it is also true that the chair you are sitting on is mostly nothing-

A high-sensitivity rare-gas mass spectrometer at Brookhaven National Laboratory. It is capable of detecting as little as one-billionth of a cubic millimeter of gas. It is used in the study of the age of meteorites.

ness, held together by the force of whirling electrons moving so rapidly that they cannot be crushed. No wonder the Bible says that the things that appear are made of things not seen.

*The Origin & Complexity of Life*

Where did life come from? Was it created by God as the Bible tells us, or did it just happen? Let's look at some of the reasons why it seems unlikely that life began by chance. First, consider what the bio-chemists are doing in the laboratory these days in their efforts to create life in a test tube.

They have made remarkable strides in producing tiny molecules. They do this by passing electric charges through various chemical solutions. The resulting molecules are far too small and simple to carry life, but they are a step, and someday perhaps they will be able to do it.

(A much asked question in science

classrooms these days is: "If scientists can create living matter in a test tube, doesn't this rule out the existence of God?" Why need it rule out any such thing? Who started this strange question, and who checked its logic? For example: If my father builds a house, and I watch how he does it, and do some experimentation and research and build one myself, does this prove that my father doesn't exist? The logic is the same.)

And now we come to the structure of the simplest form of living matter, the cell (see illustration). As you can see, it is not, after all, very simple! For a cell to be formed by chance, millions of complex protein molecules would have to "spontaneously generate" simultaneously and then by strict accident and chance join together and form into various parts of a protozoa or other single-celled unit, including such parts as the extremely complicated chromosomes and genes: otherwise, the cell could not duplicate and redup-

A diagram of a "simple" cell! Incredibly complex "machines," far more sophisticated than the most advanced data-processing mechanisms, are in every cell. In the nucleus are the chromosomes containing the coded DNA that specifies every aspect of the growth of the body. A teaspoonful of DNA is estimated to have an information capacity equal to a modern computer with a volume of 100 cubic miles!

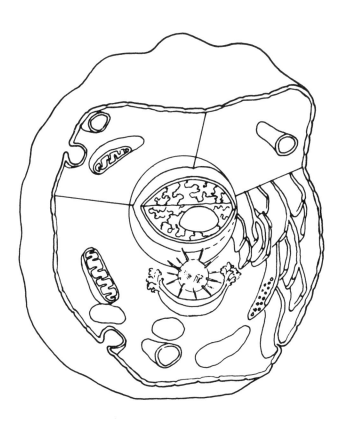

licate itself over and over again billions of times to form a human body or other form of living matter. Notice that this division of cells is not the least haphazard: an embryo within its mother is not a shapeless mass, but a shaped foetus; and the foetus continues to change. The ever-dividing cells form themselves into the digestive system, respiratory, circulatory, and so on, until the original cell has become the incredible complexity of a man or a woman.

Then, at a certain point, there are no further significant changes in the unborn child except in size. How do the cells know when to differentiate into organs and when to stop growing? Who made the chromosomes and genes that seem to be the controls? And how do these controls work?

Let me further describe how complex a cell is; for my purpose is to try to convince the open-minded that no amount of chance would form a cell, and that a Creator is required.

How new cells are formed: By the process of mitosis, the chromosomes divide and pass across spindles to form the nucleus of two new cells. Each cell of the body thus contains the identical code of every other cell in that body. This basic pattern of reproduction is not the work of chance mutations, but of the Creator.

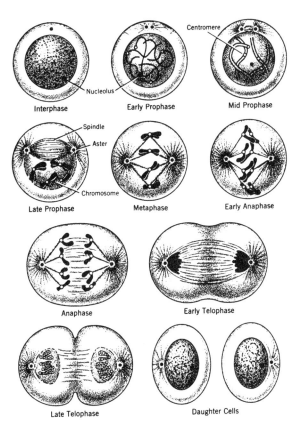

Interphase

Early Prophase

Centromere

Nucleolus

Mid Prophase

Spindle

Aster

Chromosome

Late Prophase

Metaphase

Early Anaphase

Anaphase

Early Telophase

Late Telophase

Daughter Cells

A model of the complicated DNA molecule, which is part of every cell and is the machine that manufactures proteins from raw materials.

Have you been reading about DNA? (The letters stand for deoxyribonucleic acid.) DNA is the "machine" in the chromosome of the cell that duplicates

the chromosome, including all the hereditary features to be passed on to the daughter cell whenever cell division occurs. That is, the DNA controls the color of your eyes, the shape of your body, your personality, and a million other facts about you that are different from a dog or horse, or from another person. And the DNA in each cell of the dog or horse gives those animals their special characteristics that cause them to be what they are and not a different sort of being.

How does DNA duplicate its information and how does it pass it on to its daughter cells?

DNA is a complex molecule built in the form of a double spiral, or helix (see illustration). The two backbones

are long chains of alternating sugar and phosphate groups. These two backbones are joined by four kinds of connecting rods, A, T, G and C, appearing in various sequences. In fact, so many sequences are possible that it is estimated that there are at least 4 or 5 <u>billion</u> different kinds of DNA molecule combinations in the forty-six chromosomes of man, each controlling one of his features. (It's the same idea as in a dictionary— thousands of different words and meanings come from twenty-six letters in various sequences.) It is estimated that if one could collect a teaspoon of DNA, it would have an information capacity equal to a modern computer with a volume of 100 cubic miles!

How does DNA get its message across? That is, how does the code it contains direct the various cellular processes? The illustration (page 34) makes it clear: The large mass in the illustration is a ribosome, a sort of protein factory floating in the cell. The "master plan" DNA in the chromosome (not

DNA again. This diagram shows how the DNA molecule splits apart during cell division.

shown) has already made a copy of itself on a messenger strand of RNA. This strand is open at one side so that the "manufacturing mechanism" can mesh into it (see illustration). The RNA messenger enters the ribosome like a ticker tape. Another kind of RNA, called transfer RNA, acts like the machines in the factory, putting the raw materials together in a special pattern as they follow the ticker tape directions! One end of the transfer molecule has bases that exactly match one of the three-letter words on the messenger. The other end will match only one certain kind of amino acid, a raw material of protein. Each transfer molecule, therefore, can bring in its particular amino acid only when the messenger calls for it. The amino acid molecules link and react with each other to form a particular chain of protein, one of 100,000 varieties, just as we can spell thousands of words with twenty-six letters. But "somebody" has to know how to spell!

This diagram shows how the DNA code within every cell directs the manufacture of proteins from its "tape," which is inherited and reproduced generation after generation.

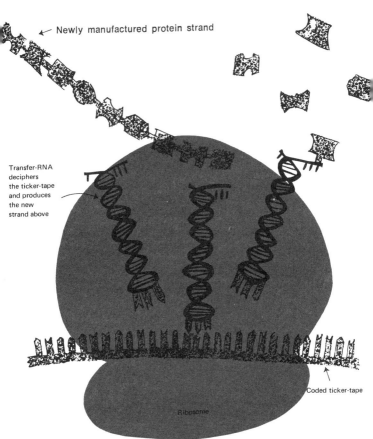

← Newly manufactured protein strand

Transfer-RNA deciphers the ticker-tape and produces the new strand above

Coded ticker-tape

Ribosome

The protein factory in every cell

As the messenger strand emerges from the other side of the "factory," it feeds into other ribosomes to direct the formation of more protein. In this way thousands of protein strips are produced in a single minute from just one strip of messenger RNA.

We have only given a summary of one part of one process in the life of a cell. We have not discussed countless other processes, such as how food comes and goes, how enzymes act as "traffic directors" to stop and start each of the operations, how a single cell or group of cells initiates the process of differentiation. Why doesn't an embryo which begins growth by single cell division simply become an adult-size embryo, rather than an organism with specialized tissues and organs? These life processes, according to some theories, arose by the chance combination of raw materials, without any participation by God. What is your opinion?

The study of instinct is not only fascinating, but wonderfully instructive concerning the relationship of God to His creation.

Now we turn to another area of
life to observe amazing things that
could not "just happen" by chance in
nature. Take a look at the world of
the ants.

Ants live in colonies, for their
duties and talents are so specific and
varied that it is a case of "all or none."
They must have each other's support
and help—or perish. Some collect food
and bring it back to the nest. Others
enlarge the nest-home or keep the rooms
clean. Still others take care of the
queens and the growing ants. Nurse-
ants have the special duty of cleaning
and feeding the larvae. Also, they move
the larvae to different parts of the nest
if the nursery becomes too wet or cold.

Where does the instinct come from,

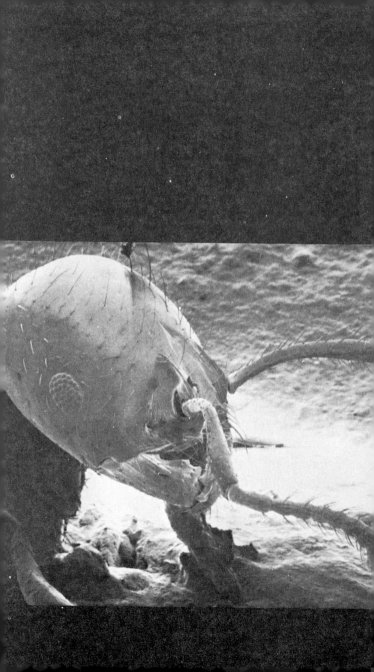

The amazing societies of ants and bees cannot reasonably be attributed to natural processes such as mutations and natural selection. It is much more reasonable to say that their instincts are God-given.

and what is instinct, that one ant should **47** perform one task and another a different task, and not all choose the same task?

Some ants are slave keepers and cannot live without slaves because their jaws are so long and sharp and curved that they cannot dig nests or feed themselves. Without their slave ants to help them, they die. How did this clumsy mutation survive? How did this "negative survival of the fittest" occur? It was apparently not by accident and chance!

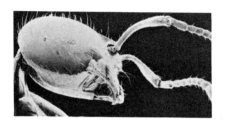

The worker ant's responsibility is to provide food, mainly wood or grass. Soldiers protect the columns of ants who go out at night to cut grass in quarter inch lengths and bring it back and stack it in storage chambers. These soldiers make up about five percent of the group. They have protruding mandibles, with a nozzle in the head for squirting chemicals at the enemy; they throw out a gummy substance that tangles the legs and antennae of the enemy and irritates its body. If their

nest is attacked, the workers begin
sealing off tunnels leading to the outside, cementing the new fragments of
soil into place with feces.

 When the  queen ant  becomes
sterile, (at that time and not before),
one of the young females starts developing the ability to mate and take over
egg production.  To say that this is all
"by instinct" is apparently true, but
who gave the instinct?

Perhaps these facts are meaningful.
Perhaps these things did not just happen.
Perhaps God with supreme intelligence
and power designed and created ants,
bees, homing pigeons and all the other
amazing assortment of creatures exhibit-
ing such common instincts as mating,
running away, migrating, etc.

The leaf-cutter ants don't eat leaves, but fungus, which is their only food. These ants use the leaves to make subterranean compost piles where their fungus farms flourish. When a virgin queen of the leaf cutters sets out on her mating flight, never to return to her old colony, she always takes with her a small piece of fungus from the colony's fungus patch. She carries this with her in a special little pocket beneath her mouth. After she has mated and shut herself up in an underground cell, she at once starts a fungus garden, planting the piece of fungus she has brought with her, fertilizing it with her own excrement, thus growing enough food to nourish herself and the first few tiny workers that hatch from her eggs. Since fungus is the only food of this kind of ant, she would starve if she forgot to carry some with her. The habits of this queen ant offer one of the many interesting and questionable points about the evolutionary theory of natural selection. For if the

theory is true, the idea of carrying along the fungus must, of necessity, have mutated simultaneously with the idea of the mating flight. It seems unlikely that such a complex set of ideas could evolve. It seems more likely that her habits arise from a God-given instinct. Incidentally, the pocket in the queen's mouth for carrying the fungus would have had to mutate simultaneously with the idea. This idea of carrying along a piece of fungus is indeed very foresighted of the queen ant, since she has never been away from the nest and has to think through in advance the strange conditions that are before her.

52

Ants make good dairy farmers! A great many different ants are interested in the small sap suckers (aphids) because of the sweet liquids they excrete; these are their "cows"! Foraging ants frequently come across groups of these aphids that have settled on some leaf or juicy shoot and sunk their stylets into the tissues of the plant. As these

insects feed, they excrete waste products which either fall to the ground or accumulate on the leaves as a sticky coating. This is known as honey-dew, and the ants, with their liking for sweet substances, are very eager to gather it up. When an ant strokes an aphid with its feet and antennae the aphid exudes a drop of this lovely liquor. The more the aphid is stroked, the more honey-dew it produces and the better it thrives, for its rate of metabolism is increased. It grows faster and reproduces better when it is kept clean by the ants.

Wood ants keep herds of aphids in underground chambers where they are fed on roots. Many ants build special shelters for their "herds." Sometimes these "barns" are made of fine grains of soil cemented together. The tropical weaver ants build special silk tents for their "cattle." It was a great day for the aphids when, somewhere down the line, an ant hatched with this interesting talent of being able to make "silk" tents for aphids!

In addition to using aphids to milk honey-dew, some varieties of ants also slaughter some of their "cattle" for meat.

Ants, like bees, when a large amount of food has been discovered, perform a kind of dance to tell each other about the direction and the distance of the good source of food!  Then their companions set out at once and go directly to it without hesitation!

Aphid milking is one of the choice tasks.  Specialists remain in charge for many weeks before taking a furlough. "Cowboy" ants stand guard to protect the herd and to keep it from straying. Dairymaids  do the milking while special "tank-car" ants (unrefrigerated, though!) carry home the honey-dew from the "barn" by filling their crops with it and disgorging it again at the nest.

The tropical weaver ants have "learned" to use the silk produced by their larvae.  The mother holds her larva in her jaws, and using it like a shuttle, passes it back and forth between the edges of several leaves, thus making a network of tiny silk threads, which draws the leaves together and forms a nest with roof and walls.

Ants are usually vicious fighters and if their homes are attacked by other ants and there is no nearby nest to move into, they will defend themselves with great vigor. But if there are other nests, they will abandon their home to the invader and move. Other ants from nearby ant hills will often come to the assistance of their friends in trouble, helping the refugees move their broods to safety. And who decides whether to attack and when to defend or whether to move? If the raided nest is small and weak the whole military operation may be completed in a matter of hours but sometimes the raiders return each afternoon, day after day, until all defense is broken down and the attackers take over the nest.

A single hive of one kind of bee can swarm as many as thirty times in one season. The bees "decide" in advance how many young queens to raise, often depending on the severity of the preceding winter.

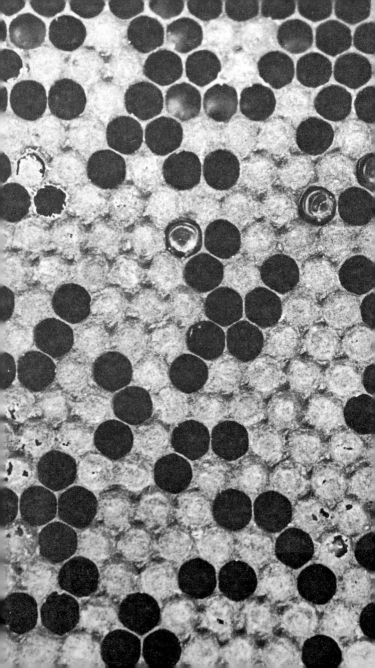

Bees, like ants, work together. Their instinct for division of labor inside and outside the hive is difficult to understand and wonderful to see.

A single hive of one kind of bee can swarm as many as thirty times in one season, sending out thirty new colonies. After an especially severe winter the bees "decide" to raise more young queens in order to replace colonies that may have died out under the severe conditions. These swarms are possible only if there is an extra queen to lead them. The new queens (usually only as many of them develop as are needed for the available swarms) are developed by the workers by overfeeding the larvae. Who makes this decision as to how many swarms there are going to be, and how many queens should be developed?

The queen ant, as soon as her mating flight takes place, breaks off her wings because she realizes (!) that she will never need them again throughout

her long life ahead; they would only
be in the way.

These, then, are some of the wonders
of creation, showing the interesting
ways God has taught the animal world
to care for itself; ways that are similar
to human ways, but apparently without
intelligence and thought.

The vast worlds above us and the
incredible worlds at our feet are evi-
dences to the open-minded of inconceivable intelligence and power. But
without open-mindedness, the strongest
evidence will fail, for "there are none
so blind as those who will not see."
To those willing to believe, the glory
of the heavens and the infinite grandeur
and order of the atomic world, and the
strange, improbable world of nature,
all point to the infinite God of creation.
How else can these facts be explained?
And it is this same all-powerful Creator
of ours who loves us and longs for us
to love Him with our entire lives—
spirit, souls and bodies. What is your
reply to Him?

**NOTES**